*Original edition published in English
under the title* The Greatest Is Love
*by Lion Publishing, England;
copyright* © *1982. All rights reserved.*
ISBN: 0-86683-688-8 (previously ISBN: 0-86760-366-6)

Compiled by Ruth Connell

1 Corinthians 13 quoted from The Holy Bible, New
International Version: *copyright* © *New York
International Bible Society, 1978*

Other Bible quotations from:
Authorized King James Version *of the Bible, Crown
copyright.*
Revised Standard Version, *copyright 1946 and
1952, second edition 1971, Division of Christian
Education, National Council of the Churches of
Christ in the USA*

*Printed and bound in Great Britain by
Purnell and Sons (Book Production) Ltd,
Paulton, Bristol*
5 4 3 2 1

THE GREATEST IS LOVE

1 Corinthians 13

Winston Press

If I speak in the tongues of men and of angels, but have not love, I am only a resounding gong or a clanging cymbal. If I have the gift of prophecy and can fathom all mysteries and all knowledge, and if I have a faith that can move mountains, but have not love, I am nothing. If I give all I possess to the poor and surrender my body to the flames, but have not love, I gain nothing.

Love is patient, love is kind. It does not envy, it does not boast, it is not proud. It is not rude, it is not self-seeking, it is not easily angered, it keeps no record of wrongs. Love does not delight in evil but rejoices with the truth. It always protects, always trusts, always hopes, always perseveres.

Love never fails. But where there are prophecies, they will cease; where there are tongues, they will be stilled; where there is knowledge, it will pass away. For we know in part and we prophesy in part, but when perfection comes, the imperfect disappears. When I was a child, I talked like a child, I thought like a child, I reasoned like a child. When I became a man, I put childish ways behind me. Now we see but a poor reflection; then we shall see face to face. Now I know in part; then I shall know fully, even as I am fully known.

And now these three remain: faith, hope and love. But the greatest of these is love.

1 Corinthians 13

If I speak in the tongues of men and of angels, but have not love, I am only a resounding gong or a clanging cymbal.

Jesus says: 'If you love me, you will keep my commandments' (John 14:15).
We cannot love our neighbour, unless we love Jesus.
We cannot love Jesus, unless we obey him.
Only the one who really loves is able to obey.
Only the one who obeys is really able to love.
'And his commandments are not burdensome' (1 John 5:3).
Walter Trobisch

Love of man necessarily arises out of the love of God. The love of the creature is but the corollary to the love of the Creator. This is what the Christian finds, as a matter of fact. His heart is overcharged with love to God. It finds its way out in love to man.

John Hooper

God is love, and love lives where God is let in.
Birgitta Yavari

If I have the gift of prophecy and can fathom all mysteries and all knowledge, and if I have a faith that can move mountains, but have not love, I am nothing.

Knowledge alone is a like a winter sun, which hath no heat or influence; it doth not warm the affections, or purify the conscience.
Thomas Watson

Man has a natural desire for knowledge, but what is the good of knowledge without the fear of God? A humble ignorant man who serves God is better than a proud scholar who observes the movements of the heavens and never gives a thought to his soul. A man who really knows his own nature sets no value on himself, and takes no pleasure in being praised by men. Even if I know everything in the world, if I do not have love, what good will it do me in the presence of God, who will judge me by what I have done?
Thomas à Kempis

Knowledge is one thing, virtue is another.
John Henry Newman

Where love is not, there is nothing that pleaseth God. For that one should love another, is all that God requireth of us; and therefore, if we desire spiritual gifts, he teacheth these gifts to be desired that help our neighbours.
William Tyndale

If I give all I possess to the poor and surrender my body to the flames, but have not love, I gain nothing.

Our Lord does not care so much for the importance of our works as for the love with which they are done.
Teresa of Avila

It is the intention that makes the gift valuable or poor, and gives to things their value.
Ambrose

If there be no love in what men do, then there is no true respect to God or men in their conduct; and if so, then certainly there is no sincerity.
Jonathan Edwards

What the poor need, Mother Teresa is fond of saying, even more than food and clothing and shelter (though they need these, too, desperately), is to be wanted. It is the outcast state their poverty imposes upon them that is the most agonizing. She has a place in her heart for them all. To her, they are all children of God, for whom Christ died, and so deserving of all love . . . Her love for them, reflecting God's love, makes them equal, as brothers and sisters within a family are equal, however widely they differ in intellectual and other attainments, in physical beauty and grace.
Malcolm Muggeridge writing about Mother Teresa

I learned that there is a giving to serve others and there is a giving to serve oneself. There is a giving to promote and a giving to dominate. But without love, there is only paternalism and self-importance.
Kefa Sempangi

You can give without loving, but you cannot love without giving.
Amy Carmichael

Love is patient

Patience is a bitter plant but it bears sweet fruit.
German proverb

'Charity', or love . . . the love of our neighbour as Christ hath loved us, 'suffereth long': is patient towards all men: it suffers all the weakness, ignorance, errors, infirmities, all the frowardness and littleness of faith, of the children of God; all the malice and wickedness of the children of the world. And it suffers all this, not only for a time, for a short season, but to the end; still feeding our enemy when he hungers; if he thirst, still giving him drink; thus continually 'heaping coals of fire', of melting love, 'upon his head'.
John Wesley

Where there is patience and humility, there is neither anger nor vexation.
St Francis of Assisi

Patience and diligence, like faith, remove mountains.
William Penn

14

Love is kind

Kindness . . . breaks up into two parts, good will and liberality. Kindness to exist in perfection must consist of these two qualities. It is not enough just to wish well; we must also do well.

Ambrose

That best portion of a good man's life,
his little, nameless, unremembered acts
of kindness and of love.

William Wordsworth

Love of God is expressed not in words but in actions.

St Theodosius

The law of love does not only pertain to the sizeable profits, but from ancient days God has commanded us to remember it in the small kindnesses of life.

John Calvin

At the times when you cannot see God, there is still open to you this sacred possibility, to show God; for it is the love and kindness of human hearts through which the divine reality comes home to men whether they name it or not.

George Merriman

He who is kind to the poor lends to the Lord,
and he will repay him for his deed.
Proverbs 19:17

Kindness, being love in its briefer contacts, must never be for
anything—except for itself alone.
W. E. Sangster

It does not envy

Rejoice with those who rejoice.

Romans 12:15

The man who has true and perfect love does not seek his own advantage in anything, but desires only that God may be glorified in all things. He feels no envy towards anyone, because he has no desire for any pleasure that is not shared.

Thomas à Kempis

Charity suppresses envy. It is not grieved at the good of others, neither of their gifts nor at their good qualities, their homes nor their estates. If we love our neighbour we shall be so far from envying his welfare . . . that we shall share in it and rejoice.

Matthew Henry

It does not boast, it is not proud

He loves but little who tells how much he loves.
John Boys

So long as we are suffering from an exaggerated sense of our own importance we can never really love our neighbours: love of one's neighbour remains something vague and abstract.
Dietrich Bonhoeffer

There are many ways of manifesting pride; and love is incompatible with them all. Love is concerned rather to give itself than to assert itself.
Leon Morris

Christians ought to imagine themselves in the place of the person who needs their help, and they ought to sympathize with him as though they themselves were suffering . . . Heartfelt pity will banish arrogance and reproach, and will prevent contempt and domineering over the poor and the needy.
John Calvin

Because God is righteous there is no true worship of him that is not immediately reflected in the love and service of our neighbour in society. Our love and service of our neighbour, however, will be saved from being patronizing or possessive as in the doing of it we are humbled by God's forgiveness and by our knowing that God's glory is the goal of what we are trying to do.
Michael Ramsey

It is not rude

He who had this love in his heart would work no evil to his neighbour. It was impossible for him, knowingly and designedly, to do harm to any man. He was at the greatest distance from cruelty and wrong, from any unjust or unkind action. With the same care did he 'set a watch before his mouth, and keep the door of his lips', lest he should offend in tongue, either against justice, or against mercy or truth. He put away all lying, falsehood, and fraud; neither was guile found in his mouth. He spake evil of no man; nor did an unkind word ever come out of his lips.

John Wesley

Rudeness is putting people down in order to try to hold ourselves up . . . Love is never rude, because love is the power that moves us toward people for their good alone.

Lewis Smedes

A soft answer turns away wrath, but a harsh word stirs up anger.

Proverbs 15:1

22

It is not self-seeking

Love seeks not its own, love gives itself wholly.
Andrew Murray

Pray for love. It is a fire — feed it — fan it. Neglected it will soon die out. Stir it up by exercise every day. Self-seeking will extinguish it before you realize what has happened.
Catherine Bramwell-Booth

The greatest thing that can happen to any human soul is to become utterly filled with love; and self-sacrifice is love's natural expression.
William Temple

Love of neighbour is not concerned about its own; it considers not how great or humble, but how profitable and needful the works are for neighbour or community.
Martin Luther

Self-pity is a cancer which erodes not only our courage and our will to happiness, but also our humanity and our capacity to love.
Mary Craig

Christianity is un-natural. It is supernatural. It is nothing less than the imparting of God's own love to our selfish hearts. When that transformation takes place, it is bound to make a difference. 'Let us not love in word or in speech, but in deed and in truth,' says the apostle John.
Michael Green

Divine Gift-love — Love Himself working in a man — is wholly disinterested and desires what is simply best for the beloved . . . Divine Gift-love in the man enables him to love what is not naturally lovable; lepers, criminals, enemies, morons, the sulky, the superior and the sneering.

C. S. Lewis

So if there is any encouragement in Christ, any incentive of love, any participation in the Spirit, any affection and sympathy, complete my joy by being of the same mind, having the same love, being in full accord and of one mind. Do nothing from selfishness or conceit, but in humility count others better than yourselves. Let each of you look not only to his own interests, but also to the interests of others.

Philippians 2:1—4

What is pure love? That which gives and gives and never demands.

Evelyn Underhill

It is not easily angered

The invitation to turn our natural loves into Charity (Divine Gift-love) is never lacking. It is provided by those frictions and frustrations that meet us in all of them; unmistakable, unless we are blinded by egotism . . . But in everyone, and of course in ourselves, there is that which requires forbearance, tolerance, forgiveness. The necessity of practising these virtues first sets us, forces us, upon the attempt to turn — more strictly, to let God turn — our love into Charity. These frets and rubs are beneficial. It may even be that where there are fewest of them the conversion of natural love is most difficult. When they are plentiful the necessity of rising above it is obvious.
C. S. Lewis

Do not repay evil with evil or insult with insult, but with blessing.
1 Peter 3:9

They that love God as they ought, will have such a sense of his wonderful long-suffering toward them under the many injuries they have offered to them, that it will seem to them but a small thing to bear with the injuries that have been offered to them by their fellow-men.
Jonathan Edwards

Love does not yield to provocation; it triumphs over all.
John Wesley

It keeps no record of wrongs

Do not seek revenge or bear a grudge against one of your people, but love your neighbour as yourself.

Leviticus 19:18

Of love there be two principal offices, one to give, another to forgive.

John Boys

An overflowing love which seeks nothing in return, agape, is the love of God operating in the human heart. At this level, we love men not because we like them, not because their ways appeal to us, nor even because they possess some type of divine spark; we love every man because God loves him. At this level, we love the person who does the evil deed, although we hate the deed that he does.

Martin Luther King Jnr

Judge not, and you will not be judged; condemn not, and you will not be condemned.

Luke 6:37

A Christian man will reckon it better to be imposed upon by his own kindness and easy temper, than to wrong his brother by an unfriendly suspicion.

John Calvin

Love stands in the presence of a fault with a finger on her lips.
Charles Haddon Spurgeon

Good to forgive;
Best, to forget!
Robert Browning

Love does not delight in evil but rejoices with the truth

A joyful heart is the normal result of a heart burning with love. Never let anything so fill you with sorrow as to make you forget the joy of Christ Risen.

Mother Teresa

Love rejoices with the truth which is Jesus Christ, and rejoicing with Christ we revel in reality as it is meant to be. We are glad to be alive in a world where truth can be known uniquely as the reality that is Jesus Christ. Evil is anything that hurts people needlessly. Christ came to save people from evil, so rejoicing in evil and rejoicing with truth are absolute antitheses.

Lewis Smedes

Whatever is true, whatever is honourable, whatever is just, whatever is pure, whatever is lovely, whatever is gracious, if there is any excellence, if there is anything worthy of praise, think about these things.

Philippians 4:8

A man of love . . . enjoys whatsoever brings glory to God, and promotes peace and goodwill among men.

John Wesley

*I*t always protects

Beareth all things . . .
King James Version

Bear one another's burdens.
Galatians 6:2

There is no conceivable combination of circumstances in which it is not possible to show love.
William Temple

Love means to love that which is unlovable, or it is no virtue at all.
G. K. Chesterton

If everyone were perfect, we should have nothing to bear from other people for the sake of God. As it is, he has made things the way they are so that we may learn to bear the burden of one another's failings. There is no one free from weakness, no one without a load to carry, no one who is self-sufficient, no one who can dispense with others' help; and so it is our duty to support each other, to comfort each other, to help, guide and advise each other.
Thomas à Kempis

Love not only begets love, it transmits strength.
Sheldon Vanauken

Always trusts, always hopes

The entry of Jesus into the heart vastly widens the scope of love. In place of suspicion and a bias to believe the worst of others, there come the most compassionate thoughts and a readiness to believe the best. Evil gossip cannot live with this love . . . The heart swells with a desire to help and all the nobler possibilities of human nature are in view. Love is like that . . . 'always eager to believe the best'.

W. E. Sangster

Love moves us to believe that every person is of great worth . . . Love just sees more than the honest eye can see. Love sees the person beneath the facts, the hardest facts, about him. And love believes that that person is of inestimable worth, is redeemable, and can become good.

Lewis Smedes

Love will not be barred by criticism, nor bound by custom . . . It seeks out its ends with a wisdom and patience that do not recognize failure as such, and finds some new reason for hope in every disappointment.

Catherine Bramwell-Booth

*A*lways *perseveres*

For love nothing is too hard. Love never speaks of sacrifice.
Andrew Murray

Love, too, will light the night of your own heart's weariness when you are alone and tempted; when you have toiled and are slighted; when your flesh is weak, and you feel forgotten by God himself . . .
Catherine Bramwell-Booth

Love always has a way to help and protect, even in its greatest affliction.
Basilea Schlink

Love even if you are not loved in return.
Richard Wurmbrand

It is better never to begin a good work than, having begun it, to stop.
Venerable Bede

Let us not become weary in doing good, for at the proper time we will reap a harvest if we do not give up.
Galatians 6:9

Love never fails. But where there are prophecies, they will cease; where there are tongues, they will be stilled; where there is knowledge, it will pass away. For we know in part and we prophesy in part, but when perfection comes, the imperfect disappears.

Knowledge, it shall cease . . . it shall cease because the perfect will absorb into itself the imperfect, as the inrushing tide will obliterate the little pools in the rocks on the seashore.
Alexander MacLaren

Love is not love
Which alters when it alteration finds,
Or bends with the remover to remove:
O, no! it is an ever-fixed mark,
That looks on tempests and is never shaken;
It is the star to every wandering bark,
Whose worth's unknown, although his height be taken.
William Shakespeare

Goodness and love are as real as their terrible opposites, and, in truth, far more real . . . But love is the final reality; and anyone who does not understand this, be he writer or sage, is a man flawed in wisdom.
Sheldon Vanauken

Who says Christianity does not make a difference? The love revolution is the greatest power in the world.
Michael Green

When I was a child, I talked like a child, I thought like a child, I reasoned like a child. When I became a man, I put childish ways behind me. Now we see but a poor reflection; then we shall see face to face. Now I know in part; then I shall know fully, even as I am fully known.

The present state is a state of childhood, the future that of manhood . . . Such is the difference between earth and heaven . . . How naturally old men, when reason is ripened and matured, despise and relinquish their infant thoughts, put them away, regret them, esteem them as nothing! Thus shall we think of our most valued gifts and acquisitions in this world when we come to heaven.
Matthew Henry

And now these three remain: faith, hope and love. But the greatest of these is love.

Many waters cannot quench love; rivers cannot wash it away.
Song of Solomon 8:7

Faith, hope and love are the three principal graces, of which charity is the chief, being the end to which the other two are but means.
Matthew Henry

Heaven is the perfection of persons in selfless love with one another and with God.
Michael Ramsey

Prayer

Jesus,
I come to you
because once again I am unable to love.

I have often produced love
within myself
but it never lasts.

I am coming to you
to be filled with your love
which reaches so much deeper than my love.

I am totally dependent
on the gift of your love,
the fruit of the Holy Spirit.

I can do so little,
only expose myself to your transforming love:
make me capable of loving.
Ulrich Schaffer

Quotations from copyright material are as follows:
Dietrich Bonhoeffer, Letters and Papers from
Prison, *edited by Eberhard Bethge, translated by*
Reginald H. Fuller, SCM Press 1953; Mary Craig,
Blessings, *Hodder and Stoughton 1979; Michael*
Green, What is Christianity?, *Lion Publishing*
1981; Thomas à Kempis, The Imitation of Christ,
translated by Betty I. Knott, Collins Fontana 1963;
Martin Luther King Jnr, Strength to Love, *Harper*
and Row 1963, Hodder and Stoughton 1964; C. S.
Lewis, The Four Loves, *Collins Fontana 1963;*
Leon Morris, 1 Corinthians, *Tyndale Press 1958;*
Malcolm Muggeridge, Something Beautiful for
God, *Collins 1971; Kefa Sempangi,* A Distant
Grief, *Regal Books USA 1979, published in UK as*
Reign of Terror, Reign of Love, *Lion Publishing*
1979; Ulrich Schaffer, Love Reaches Out, *Harper*
and Row 1976, Lion Publishing 1976; Lewis
Smedes, Love within Limits, *William B. Eerdmans*
Publishing Company 1978, Lion Publishing 1979;
William Temple, in Daily Readings from William
Temple, *compiled by Hugh C. Warner, Hodder and*
Stoughton 1948; Mother Teresa, quoted in
Something Beautiful for God *by Malcolm*
Muggeridge, Collins 1971; Sheldon Vanauken, A
Severe Mercy, *Hodder and Stoughton 1977; Walter*
Trobisch, Love is a Feeling to be Learned, *Editions*
Trobisch 1971, Inter-Varsity Press 1974; Birgitta
Yavari, There is a Love, *Interbook Publishing 1972,*
first published in Sweden by Bonniers under the title
Det finns en kärlek

Photographs by Sonia Halliday Photographs: Sonia
Halliday, pages 9, 15, F. H. C. Birch page 11; Lion
Publishing: David Alexander, pages 17, 19, 25, 29,
33, 41 and cover, Jon Willcocks, pages 13, 20, 23,
27, 35, 37, 38, 43; Jean-Luc Ray, page 30